ALL THE YESTERDAY'S AFTER

SELECTED HAIKU

STEFANIE BENNETT

IT IS BETTER TO HAVE LESS

THUNDER IN THE MOUTH

AND MORE LIGHTNING

IN THE HAND

(Native American Proverb)

ACKNOWLEDGEMENTS

Some of these poems have been published in the following:

Poems from The Paddy Wagon – The Medium – Shade - One Plus Two

The North Brisbane College of Advanced Education – Dead Snakes

Shot Glass Journal – Cosh – UFO Gigolo – Tomato Press – Khasmik Poets

Stanzaic Stylings – Whispers – Standing Rock – Kind of a Hurricane Press

High Coupe – Record Magazine – Poetry Super Highway – Haiku Universe

The Australian – World Haiku Series 2019 – Akita International Haiku Network

And others…

Cover Photo : Tania Kavney

Rear Photo : Stefanie Bennett

Once again, a very large thankyou to those who have supported my work of words over the last few years. I thank you for the time you have given me. Also, in 2007, the coming together of Australian Groups ie; the ACF, CFA, Arts Action for Peace and others, joined the call for a 'nuclear free world'.

ICAN – The International Campaign to Abolish Nuclear Weapons was born. I am proud of and indebted to my lot for having won the 2017 Nobel Peace Prize.

ABOUT THE AUTHOR

Stefanie Bennett, has published over a dozen volumes of poetry, a libretto and a novel. She has tutored in The Institute of Modern Languages (James Cook University), acted as a published editor…and worked with [No Nukes] Arts Action for Peace.

Of mixed heritage (Irish/Italian/Paugussett-Shawnee), she was born in QLD Australia in 1945. Stefanie, an ex-blues singer and musician, has been fluent internationally in poetry online and in print journals. She has been nominated for the Best of the Net and The Pushcart.

TIME-LINE QUOTES

Beyond Bennett's undoubted technical skills however, is the quality, which elevates her to the top rank of Australian poets.

(Tim Thorne)

If we frame her as a surrealist following poets like Eluard and Aragon, we are able to view those symbols as expressions of some notion of true life.

(Simon Eales)

Stefanie Bennett – I believe the poetry content matter is rattling magnificent.

(Poetry Pacific: Zem Karlos)

After 'Wen and The Red Candle'. This superb poem is not only beautifully written, but also all the more remarkable for capturing a very Asian poetic voice, despite being written in a distinctly 'western' style.

(Robert Lavett Smith)

YESTERDAY

A cicada chorus sings
the song
of memento

FORGET-ME-NOTS

Naming names the penny
drops
occasionally

RECKLESS

Ants on my pillow:
sleeping with
the enemy

WINTER SOLSTICE

The jackass laughs
the willow
weeps

REVERSE MEMORY

The crow whisperer
crosses
life's fault-line

GADGETRY

Guide-dog infatuated:
the by-passing
walking-stick

POLL-TICKING

These days Genghis Khan
could be seen as
a soul man

TSUNAMI EVENT

No eagle, no cry
in the sweet
by-and-by

TROUBLE

Can looks deceive!
The full moon's
grown a handle

HUMANITIES

The cat knows – and what
does the cat say?
Impeachment USA

OVERVIEW

Busking in the rain –
the small change
musician

DEVINE COMEDY

What we do know we don't
know because it's
substantial

OLD DUTCH

Pick of the crop:
other to other
soulmates

BUSON'S VISION

Who taught the sinking
silver moon
how to swim

IMMEDIACY

Tourists photographing
the water-wheel
in Summer rain

SYNOPSIS

Why weep when the red eyed
tree frog
sings Carmen

FRAME WORK

How to paint a picture
with no-one
in it

ARRIVAL LA

Three border crossings
what state is it
I'm in…

INTRODUCTION

Memory is…
my best
friend

PEACE SPEAK

It's just the thunder
from
'down under'

INFILTRATING THE LIVING

Sliding doors –
old poets
don't die

ATTENTION

Blooming dandelions
sheltering
the sun

TRANSCRIPT

A ragamuffin's check list:
no rain
no water

REALITIES

Pawn shopping…the whole
world's at
odds and ends

RADIO NATIONAL

E-book re-written:
play it again
mam

LANDCARE

Waking up alive –
I had nothing
to do with it

SILVER LINING

Quieten up, out-riders
the tree world's
remembering

CUT AND PASTE

The vows we made –
still waters
run deep

HOUSE RULES

A bemused green ant
studying
croquet

AESTHETICS

The intimacy of one
now embraces
the sun

FOR THE RECORD

The bowling-green –
yellowing
the day

BAD TASTE

Fossil fuel's
harm
burger

SCREAM

A necessary cease
fire
North to South

SANDSTONE PASS

Stay or go, love: it's
still a life-long
Winter

CATCH AS CATCH CAN

3 legged race –
we missed
by a mile

SPIRIT MATTER

At best two falling stars:
I go out
to greet my guests

SEEN BUT ONCE

Aurora Borealis:
I get a kick
out of you

FORGOTTEN IMAGES

A dripping tap –
who sprung
the bobcat

FIELD OF DREAMS

Quite likely the planet
wanted to be
born flat

ANALYSIS

Verandah door ajar:
zazen
slips on through

ANXIETY

The lunar eclipse
just another
identity theft

WRITER'S BLOCK

A twister will
fix
it

CLOUDBURST

The endangered stranger –
a monkey
in a raincoat

NON-ATTACHMENT

All the birds in the air
a-buzz
with tanka

FORCEFUL MOVE

Enough already: stop
slam dunking
peace-talks

HOLLOWNESS

'I want to apologise' –
try instead…
"avoidance tactics"

COUNTERPOINT

A Buddhist foot-note:
prisoners
not taken

NUANCE

Ancient field plough
facing
plover's Noh cry

NON-BELIEVER

Yeshua never said
it's raining
cats & dogs

TOUCHSTONE

I heard the silence
for the last time
coming

CAUSE AND EFFECT

Sometimes the book-mark
says more than
the book

ANCHORS AWEIGH

Star gazing: an angel
balancing
on a pin head

SARAJEVO 1992

The soundless
burning
of books…

CO-EXISTENCE

Resounding thunder:
my button-hole
full of rain

SOUND PATTERN

Covered in fleas
the bespoken
dog-catcher

LEGALISED CANNABIS

Can't roll
your
own

PINE GAP AUSTRALIA

I'd rather be a tramp
than
a trumpet blower

STOP – LOOK – LISTEN

Your name is already written
on the Olivetti's
typewriter keys

ABANDONED

Hanshan goes
back to
the future

CONCORD

A tawny frogmouth owl
envelopes
the Zen garden

THE GUARDIAN

Earth's drummer –
echidna
snoring

MIDDLE CLASS

Divided
into
three

DETACHMENT

Day-break's
broken
pencil

TASMANIAN OAK

The ancient
wind
whisperer

SCRIPTURES

A blue wren's nest
speaks in tongues
of wonder

RAW PRAWN

Social media's
eye-
soar

THE TELLING IMAGE

An empty swing:
winging circles
of eight

PRO-ACTIVE

Sign reads no entry
now the gates
gone

COUNT DOWN

Two minus two
no longer
less

PURPLE RAIN ELECTION

Tanka soup
counting
coup

KEEP SAKE

A frog-full sound
without
water

AFTER-WORD

The rise and fall
of the plum
blossom

PUNCH DRUNK

Best knock: the door-knob
is yester year's
screamer

LOST AND FOUND

On the iris petal
a deceased
moon-lit letter

POD CAST

There's a mouse in the house
of each quiet
Australian

INSIGHTFUL

Geronimo! The harvest
moon's had
a face lift

COLLISION

The poem writes the poet
reading
the reader

PICNIC

A bull-ant waiting
to pass on
the mustard

DAYLIGHT

Wild weather – even
the scarecrow's
fancy dancing

FLEXIBILITY

Follow the index
not
the book

SATORI

I pick up the phone
when it stops
ringing

THE AVENGER

Sister Moon
retains
lost ground

RAIN JOURNAL

Sound of picturesque –
thunder-drums
calling

ANNOUNCEMENT

Around a weather-vane's pulse
the firefly
gathering

BRUSH TO PAPER

White haired sister –
all that growing
matters

TIMELESSNESS

Nature's hand alone
strums
the Zen of it

KUKAI, PEACE TREATY

There will be no more logs
on my
fire

ACCESS

Lunar eclipse –
hold onto
your pentacles

BURMA

A winning Nobel Laureate
wronging
what's right

PRATTLE

At home on the hockey stick
the bemused
tree frog

TELEPATHY

Love's leaky boat
the colour
of money

PERCEPTION

Walking away –
the two sided
mirror

CLASS ACTION

Being seen and
not heard
what then –

SCOTTISH HIGHLANDS

Heather in bloom
charting–
the milky way

TOURISM

Flying dutchman
detached
performance -

POCKET-BOOK BELOVED

An upside-down
island
in the sky

RESURRECTION USA

Claw hammer and nail –
go fix
the complex

STATE OF THE ART

It's the company
we did
not keep

THE CHILL

Love lost in space
clouds so long
in passing

FOR TENDER

Organically
grown
money…

STRUCK OUT

Left in storage –
freight trains
going nowhere

THE PARADOX

A barn-owl hoots
her own purring
call

HITCH HIKING

upending what's pending
the Haiku's
sisterhood

LANDSCAPE

Sometimes time
itself unveils
a strange logic

SOUL SEARCH

Loneliness stands tall
in the wind's
saddle

AVIDITY

Alice in Blunderland
seated on
The Orient Express

STORE BELOW ZERO

Getting over it –
a long train's
running

RESPECTFULLY SO

When the past is
a ghost
say "go now"

IRREPLACEABLE

Drain-pipe cricket
twilighting
thunder

WINGS OF CHANGE

Identical twins:
one brown
one yellow

ALL STOPS OUT

An alter ego exchange
for
a credit card

BOOZE BUS

Family drive through –
Grandma's
at the wheel

SAD SACK

Driven: the yellow dog
with a monkey
on its back

DRAMA

Take it or leave it –
we live in
a soap opera…

MEANS TESTING

Getting used to it
before
it happens

CONDUCT

Indian Summer –
every thing
comes undone

NUMBERS

On the day love died
the Sufi
played Gin Rummy…

AGED ODYSSEY...

Hearing the nightingale's
song
at dusk –

DISCLOSURE

Another fly-by haiku
concealed
by a storm

NIRVANA

The deceased in question
starts
sniffling

GECKO

Found cat-napping
between the oboe
and the fiddle

MISSION IMPOSSIBLE

Photos on the mantlepiece:
this one loved me
this one not –

DESIRE

The Tea Ceremony:
who's watching
who –

RAIN COURIER

Crow carries a cloud-burst
to the saltbush
on the rise

YUKON TERRITORY

The haiku I missed
is not at all
hit and miss

BACKLASH

Except for the coat-hanger –
the empty
closet

EDEN

A note-book mind –
how it brushes
the ink-stone

REUNION

And the heartbeat's
a dead
give away…

DESIGNATION

Taking her place –
the morning star's
Sierra Sunrise

THE ESSENCE

What do literacy beings do –
weed the world's
weeping gardens

SALVATION

Finding the arrow-head
after first
having found me

PASTORAL

September half-moon
tail-gating
the clouds

JOURNEY

Visiting the graves:
dewdrop spirits
one by one

WAKEFULNESS

The green tambourine
earnestly played
at age 83

BUDDHA LAND

Inside the bodhi tree
practicing
poetry

BOUNDARIES

Night-sky chatter
the third eye
matters

SOLITUDE

One without
the other's
rain check

LIGHTNING STRIKE

On the road to Kumano
the cormorant
passes through

FOR SALE

Rogue humanity –
a dime
a dozen

DEXTERITY

Troop's salad:
hit
or miss

A CONCEPT

Once the forest
went
walk-about

ALIVE

Hanging from a thorn –
the white cliffs
of Dover

TUG-O-WAR

Around the bend
the sushi
wrap…

SEARCH

Yearly pursuits
she photographs
Bora Rings

DISSENSION

Only sister moon knows
there's no East
there's no West

Develop-MENT

Great aunt…more
lines than
War and Peace

AD HOC

Capitalism is finished –
just ask
the borrowers

RESTORATION

Go now: our attachment's
written itself
into history

STATUS

At the square mile
how rare was
the round tree

VORTEX

Old woman time –
a friend
of mine

LOVE ALLIANCE

Becoming the shadow
no longer
there

PAY DIRT

Ah! The logic
of
a cork-screw

TWILIGHT

Through the window
yesterday's
paper roses